Inspired by James Allen's Motivational Classic,
"As a Man Thinketh"

AS A WOMAN THINKS

Abby Leigh Hunter

Virtual University Press

As a Woman Thinks

Copyright © 2023 Virtual University Press
First Edition: May 2023

This work is protected by United States and international copyright law. All Rights Reserved Worldwide. No part of this work may be reproduced in any manner without the publisher's express consent.

Cover image licensed from Adobe Stock Graphics and customized by the publisher. All rights reserved.

This book is available in multiple formats including Kindle, EPUB, paperback, and hardcover. Wholesale orders for paperback and hardcover editions may be placed through Ingram Content Group's iPage order system by searching for the ISBNs listed below.

Address use requests and general correspondence to the publisher by email to Editor@VU.org or use our online contact form at https://vu.org/contact-us/

ISBN Numbers:

978-1-64399-052-1	Kindle e-book
978-1-64399-056-9	EPUB e-book
978-1-64399-053-8	Retail paperback
978-1-64399-054-5	Paperback (Ingram)
978-1-64399-055-2	Hardcover (Ingram)

Table of Contents

INTRODUCTION
The Power to Transform Your Life..5

CHAPTER 1
Thought and Character: A Woman's Journey..........................15

CHAPTER 2
The Power of Thought on Circumstances................................23

CHAPTER 3
How Thought Affects Health and Body....................................39

CHAPTER 4
A Woman's Thoughts and Purpose..47

CHAPTER 5
Thought and the Pathway to Achievement.............................55

CHAPTER 6
Dreams, Visions, and Ideals..67

CHAPTER 7
Serenity..77

CHAPTER 8
Thirty Women Who Changed the World..................................83

About the Author...101

Introduction

The Power to Transform Your Life

*Y*ou are about to embark on a transformative reading experience, where you hold the key to unlock your incredible inner potential. If you have ever encountered disappointments, endured struggles in relationships, grappled with unhealthy habits, or found yourself standing at life's crossroads, the wisdom in these pages may serve as your guiding light.

In the following chapters, you will delve into the laws of thought and learn how to harness their power. You'll uncover methods to manage stress and anxiety, cultivate unshakable confidence, and replace negative thinking with a positive and confident mindset. You will learn how your thoughts influence your health, diet, sleep patterns, even your immune system and cholesterol levels. Importantly, this book will explore the unique challenges and opportunities that modern women face in their lives. It provides insightful guidance on navigating the intricacies of relationships, career advancement, self-care, and personal growth. By employing the principles discussed here, you can surmount obstacles, embrace your true potential, and craft a fulfilling life in today's ever-changing world.

As a Woman Thinks is a special edition inspired by and based on the motivational classic *As a Man Thinketh* by James Allen. Penned at the turn of the twentieth century, Allen's book has influenced millions; but its writing style is grounded in a bygone era where readers were presumed to be male, and only men and their endeavors are discussed. With thoughtful and diligent editing, this edition has been created specifically for women. It reimagines Allen's timeless wisdom and expands his core philosophies, providing insights on concerns women have in today's world. This work also draws inspiration from *As a Man Thinks: Classic Edition,* an updated version of Allen's work edited by motivational author and editor Richard De A'Morelli, with permission from the publisher. Each chapter offers insights that capture the essence of a woman's life journey, empowering you, the reader, to traverse societal expectations, gender biases, and issues of self-esteem, while learning to recognize and embrace your unique strengths and thrive in all areas of your life.

Prepare to embark on a journey that will open your eyes and heart to the extraordinary power of your mind—a power capable of moving mountains and revolutionizing your life. By harnessing the power of thought, you can shatter limitations, unleash your highest potential, and create a life of purpose, fulfillment, and empowerment.

Who Was James Allen?

James Allen was a British author, philosopher, and a trailblazer in the self-help/motivational movement of the early twentieth century. Through his writings, he crafted a legacy that continues to shape lives today. His best-known work, *As a Man Thinketh,* has motivated millions to change their lives by harnessing the power of thought. It profoundly influenced countless authors in the years that followed, giving rise to numerous bestsellers, including Norman Vincent Peale's *The Power of Positive Thinking* and Joshua Liebman's *Peace of Mind*.

Born in Leicester, England, on November 28, 1864, Allen's early years were marked by adversity. His family's business collapsed shortly after his birth, and his father's pursuit of a new start in America tragically ended with him being robbed and murdered just two days after he arrived in New York.

The loss of Allen's father plunged the family into hardship, forcing Allen to leave school and seek full-time work at the age of fifteen. He spent the next two decades employed in clerical jobs. In 1902, he took a leap of faith and left his employment to pursue writing —an improbable dream for a high school dropout. He fervently believed in the power of the mind and maintained that every individual possesses free will and the ability to shape their own destiny. The intensity of his belief put Allen onto a path that would profoundly alter his life's trajectory.

Defying skeptics, Allen achieved his unlikely dream of becoming an author, writing and publishing twenty-one inspirational books over nine years. While not driven by fame or fortune, he was able to sustain himself on modest earnings and remained firm in his belief that the universe would provide for his needs.

After publication of his first book, *From Poverty to Power*, Allen relocated to Ilfracombe, a seaside town on England's southern coast. Surrounded by picturesque rolling hills and Victorian charm, he discovered the perfect sanctuary for spiritual contemplation and writing.

Soon after his arrival in Ilfracombe, Allen wrote his second book, *As a Man Thinketh*. This seminal work embodied the essence of his belief in the power of the mind and an individual's ability to shape their own destiny. Despite initial hesitation, it was his wife, Lily, who encouraged him to submit his manuscript to a publisher. He could never have foreseen that it would become his most enduring success.

James Allen lived a modest, ascetic life modeled after the mystics portrayed in the writings of Russian novelist and philosopher Leo Tolstoy, whom Allen deeply admired. His lifestyle embraced moderation, self-discipline, respect for all living beings, and voluntary simplicity. Like Tolstoy, Allen focused on the goals of happiness, positivity, embracing the present moment, and finding the silver lining in every cloud. He was an avid learner, warmly welcomed new ideas, and embraced physical labor. He expressed gratitude for even the smallest blessings life bestowed on him, and he endeavored to express positive thoughts and actions in his daily existence.

Allen's fame as a writer and philosopher was brief, ending abruptly at the age of 47 when he passed away in his sleep. Reflecting on his life's work, his wife Lily reminisced, "He wrote when he had a message, and it became a message only when he had lived it out in his own life and knew it was good."

A proverbial messenger who delivered the right message to the world at the right time, James Allen's writings rose to prominence as the rigid doctrines of Protestantism in Europe began to ease. Blending Christianity with mystical teachings from the East, he offered an alternative to the harsh doctrine that humans are born into sin and condemned to suffer in the purgatory of Earth. Instead, he proposed an optimistic perspective that recognized the inherent goodness within individuals and the seeds of divine wisdom that reside in each of us.

As the grip of Protestant dogma began to loosen, a renewed interest in philosophy and alternative religions blossomed in the early 1900s. Science and religion found common ground, with Charles Darwin's *The Origin of Species* at the forefront. Darwin himself recognized the power of thought, writing, "The highest possible stage in moral culture is when we recognize that we ought to control our thoughts."

Allen's writings on the power of thought and free will have empowered millions of readers, affirming that individuals possess the capacity for good and positive expression, while others choose negativity or evil. Every day, we have the ability to chart our own course. Our successes and failures, joys, sorrows, achievements, disappointments—all are the products, directly or indirectly, of our own thoughts and actions.

While the teachings expressed in Allen's writings are not unique or original, they carry an undeniable resonance, for as Ecclesiastes 1:9 reminds us, "There is nothing new under the sun." Drawing from diverse sources, most notably Buddhism, Allen built his philosophy of empowerment on the ancient wisdom in *The Dhammapada*, a Buddhist scripture from the third century B.C. that reveals: "All that we are is the result of what we have thought." Echoing this insight, Allen wrote: "As a man thinketh in his heart, so is he."

The writings of James Allen, and the timeless wisdom from which he drew, are today recognized as part of a broader humanist philosophy called the Science of Life. Its core teachings affirm that our thoughts have the power to shape our reality. Every thought, every action, creates a ripple effect that obeys the law of cause and effect, shaping our conditions and experiences. Thus, every individual has the power to shape their life and control their destiny. James Allen's teachings reflect these principles, extolling the transformative potential of thought, the importance of personal responsibility, and every person's inherent power to shape their life according to their desires. By understanding how life's natural laws work in our own daily affairs, we can unlock deeper insights into the interconnectedness between our thoughts, actions, and outcomes, which in turn empowers us to create the life we truly desire.

The transformative impact of these teachings can be seen in the lives of several of my friends who had the opportunity to read a draft of *As a Woman Thinks* when I began working on this project in 2020.

Emily, a successful businesswoman, had been struggling with work-related stress and anxiety. After she understood the power of thought and the natural laws governing every aspect of life, she was able to cultivate a positive and focused mindset, which not only helped her resolve her stress issues but also propelled her to a significant job promotion. She attributes her success to the transformative impact of recognizing that she is the architect of her thoughts and destiny.

Sarah, a single mother facing financial turmoil, applied the principles of positive thinking and cause and effect to her life. Embracing the belief that she could create a better future for herself and her kids, she took control of her finances and credits the fundamental teachings of James Allen for enabling her to believe in her own power and potential.

Marina, a struggling artist, had been grappling for nearly a year with self-doubt and creative blocks. After reading my draft of *As a Woman Thinks,* she had an epic awakening, realizing that her own thoughts were inhibiting her artistic expression. By practicing positive affirmations and visualization techniques, she overcame her self-limiting attitudes and tapped into her natural creativity. Her artwork is now flourishing. Maya credits the wisdom and insights presented in this book for unlocking her artistic potential and guiding her on a path of self-discovery.

Rachel, a high-achieving professional, felt adrift in her life, despite her outward success. Reading *As a Woman Thinks* helped her shift her focus from external achievements to a search for her inner purpose. She began aligning her actions with her values and passions, which led her to a pivotal career change. She is now on a career path that harmonizes with her true calling and brings her deep satisfaction and joy.

These stories illustrate how women from various backgrounds and circumstances have positively transformed their lives by recognizing the power of thought and their own innate power to influence their future, replacing negative attitudes and conditions with a rich life of happiness and personal satisfaction.

Today, in a world rife with injustice, prejudice, suffering, and conflict, it is reassuring to know that we possess the choice to lead peaceful, harmonious, and purposeful lives. By embracing positive thoughts and actions in our daily affairs, we can manifest this transformative potential.

As we embark now on an enlightening journey through the teachings of James Allen, his message remains timeless and resonates with people of all ages and genders, and from all walks of life. This adaptation of his classic offers contemporary women a guiding compass through the complexities of modern living. Combining time-honored insights and fresh perspectives, may these words illuminate the extraordinary power of your mind and guide you in the creation of a beautiful, enriching, and fulfilling life.

Chapter 1

Thought and Character: A Woman's Journey

The ancient wisdom, "As a woman thinks in her heart, so she is," to paraphrase Proverbs 23:7, encompasses not merely her being but every condition and circumstance of her life. A woman is truly the sum and total of her thoughts, and her character is woven from the threads of her inner musings. Every delight, every challenge, every deed, every habit, and even every predicament in which she finds herself, mirror her thoughts and are born from her own creation.

Just as a flower blossoms from a seed and otherwise could not exist, every action in a woman's daily life blooms from the fertile soil of her thoughts, even those spontaneous, unplanned moments that catch her by surprise.

Thought gives birth to action, and action in turn blossoms into joy or suffering. Thus, a woman reaps what she sows. She harvests the sweet and bitter fruit of the seeds she has planted and nurtured in the rich garden of her mind and soul.

> *Thought in the mind has shaped us into what we are.*
> *By thought, a woman crafts and directs her life.*
> *If a woman's mind harbors shadows and negative thoughts,*
> *Pain follows her as the wheel trails the ox.*
> *If a woman perseveres in serene and positive thought,*
> *Joy follows her as faithfully as her own shadow.*

What you think is what you become. Your life and affairs are governed by natural laws. Nothing happens by coincidence. The law of "cause and effect" prevails in the hidden realm of thought, just as it does in the visible world of tangible things. An enlightened character cannot be gained from a book or purchased at any price, and it does not manifest overnight. It is the radiant outcome of deliberate effort and unwavering devotion to nurturing and expressing positive and harmonious thoughts. Conversely, a character marked by cruelty, malice, or rage is the inevitable outcome of persistently dwelling on dark, vengeful, and destructive thoughts.

You are sculpted or broken, and made or unmade, by your thoughts, and by the actions that sprout from those thoughts. In the workshop of the mind, you create the tools for your own growth or fashion the foundations for creating a life filled with joy, strength, and peace. By choosing empowering thoughts, making the right choices, and transforming them into action, you can reach your loftiest goals and the pinnacle of happiness. Conversely, misuse of thought, harnessing it destructively, can lead you down to the darkest depths of human nature. Between these two extremes lies the full spectrum of character, and you are the architect and builder of your own character.

Of all the beautiful truths pertaining to the soul that have been unearthed and illuminated, none are more empowering or fill the heart with more courage, hope, and confidence than this: You are the weaver of your thoughts, the shaper of your character, the initiator of your actions, and the architect of your condition, environment, and destiny.

As a woman of power, intelligence, and love, and as the creator of your own thoughts, you possess the master key to every situation in life. Within you resides a transformative and life-altering force that empowers you to shape your reality.

A woman is always the designer of her life and circumstances, even in her most vulnerable moments and her deepest despair. In those fragile moments and dark hours, she might falter, mismanaging her inner world, squandering her energies, alienating her loved ones, and dwelling in the shadows of her soul. Yet, when she turns inward to reflect upon her state and seeks to understand the laws that govern her character and environment, she becomes the wise guide, the caring and charitable force for good, the all-seeing eye of empathy and intuition, channeling her formidable energies with intelligence, and focusing her thoughts on substantial issues. In this way, she becomes the conscious architect of her character and author of her destiny. However, this transformation can only happen when she realizes that the laws of thought are at work in her life, and she learns to apply those laws wisely. Such insight comes only through profound self-reflection and experience.

Just as gold and diamonds are unearthed by diligent search and mining, so too can the truths that shape your character and circumstances be discovered by delving deep into the mines of your soul. In those caverns of your soul, you will uncover the truth: that you are the artisan of your character, the sculptor of your life, and the author of your destiny.

You can find unerring proof of these truths if you observe and alter your thoughts as you navigate the course of your daily life. Observe the effects of your thoughts on yourself and others. Notice their impact on your life and circumstances. By patient observation, you'll begin to recognize the chain of cause and effect, the intricate web that connects all events in your life. You can then use every experience, even the most trivial occurrences, as stepping stones to self-knowledge and better understanding your thought processes. From that knowledge springs the fruits of self-awareness, wisdom, and power.

By engaging in these actions and consciously living your life in accordance with the laws of thought, you will realize the unfaltering truth of the law: To the woman who asks, it shall be given; to the woman who seeks, she shall find; and to the woman who knocks, the door will be opened (Luke 11:10). Patience, practice, and unwavering application of this law will guide you on your journey towards the Temple of Knowledge.

Further Insights

In this opening chapter, a fundamental principle is introduced that will serve as the backbone for every subsequent chapter in this book:

You are what you think,
and you can change your life,
for better or worse,
by changing your thoughts.

The scale of change you can expect will depend on the effort you put into guiding your thoughts from negative to positive, and your determination to remain positive. Even small adjustments in your thought processes can lead to subtle improvements in your circumstances. If you make major changes, you will likely see immediate, gratifying progress in all aspects of your life—physical, emotional, and spiritual.

Not every woman finds her way to the path of positive consciousness described in this book. Some become entangled in negative thinking, spurred by the doubts and fears that complicate our daily lives. These detrimental thoughts surface in various forms, such as anger, insecurity, jealousy, depression, self-criticism, and harmful habits. Becoming stuck in this quagmire of negativity can send your life spiraling downwards, potentially ensnaring you in this unfortunate state for an extended time.

The phrase, "Think positive!" is often casually tossed around. You might be inclined to dismiss it as an empty platitude or a cliché lacking substance. Or perhaps you might retort, "I always think positive about achieving my goals, but they never materialize!" Merely hoping for a wonderful event is not positive thinking; it is wishful thinking, and idle thoughts never take root and bear fruit. As you delve deeper into this book, you'll learn that it requires a deep understanding of the laws of the mind, along with diligent, persistent effort, to keep your thoughts focused on the positive. It's all too easy to let doubts and fears about insignificant issues taint our thoughts, especially when we've spent years entangled in challenging situations and have come to expect setbacks and disappointment at every turn.

In his book *Live Well, Be Happy*, motivational author Richard De A'Morelli explains, "A few drops of positive energy won't have any effect if you are submerged in a swamp of negativity. This is why, when a person complains, 'I meditated and held a positive thought for five minutes!' and they see no change, they erroneously conclude that positive thinking doesn't work. For positive thoughts to bring positive results, you need to liberate yourself from the swamp and plant your feet on solid ground. Only then can you commence the process of purging negativity from your surroundings and planting seeds of positivity in your garden."

Before we proceed, let's clarify what we mean by "the power of positive thinking" and examine some of the evidence supporting its effectiveness. Contemporary psychology and the medical community offer compelling evidence that our thoughts impact us on every level: physical, emotional, intellectual, and spiritual. Even the esteemed Mayo Clinic acknowledges the benefits of positive thinking. A staff-written article published on the Mayo Clinic website states: "Is your glass half-empty or half-full? How you answer this age-old question about positive thinking may reflect your outlook on life, your attitude toward yourself, and whether you are optimistic or pessimistic —and it may even affect your health. Indeed, studies confirm that character traits like optimism and pessimism can affect many areas of your health and well-being."

The article goes on to list the proven benefits, including increased life span, lower rates of depression, reduced stress and anxiety, a better sense of well-being, lower risk of death from cardiovascular disease, and enhanced coping skills during stressful times. The exact mechanisms behind the health benefits of positive thinking are not fully understood by science, but it is clear that embracing a positive mindset can lead to a more fulfilling and empowered life.

As we navigate through our day-to-day journey in life, we must remember that positive thinking, like its negative counterpart, is a habit. It requires time and steadfast effort to develop, but can quickly erode, leading us back to old, familiar patterns if we are not mindful. So, even if you make a concerted effort and succeed in embracing positive thinking into your life, you must remain vigilant against backsliding. The climb to the mountain's peak is strenuous and challenging. A momentary slip can lead to a swift and certain descent. It simply happens, it happens quickly, and the consequences can be startling and severe.

In the next chapter, we will explore how positive thinking can influence your life, your prospects for happiness and success, and your spiritual destiny. We will delve into how embracing and nurturing a positive mindset can become a powerful ally, helping you flourish and realize your full potential as a woman, beyond stereotypical constraints. You hold an innate power to create, nurture, and transform. Tap into this power, and you can ascend the ladder of life to an existence filled with positivity and fulfillment.

Chapter 2

The Power of Thought on Circumstances

A woman's mind is like a fertile garden, and her thoughts are seeds ready to sprout. She can consciously cultivate positive and uplifting thoughts, or let her thoughts run wild. Either way, those seeds of her thoughts must and will grow. If no beneficial seeds are sown, an uncontrolled growth of unproductive thoughts will flourish, like weeds in a neglected garden, perpetuating more of the same.

Just as you would cultivate a garden, maintaining it free from weeds and nurturing the flowers you desire, so you must tend the garden of your mind, weeding out negative and disruptive thoughts, and fostering the growth of useful and positive ones. By cultivating the seeds of thought you plant, you will realize that you are the master gardener of your soul, the director of your life, and the designer of your destiny. You will begin to understand the laws of thought at work within yourself, and you'll comprehend with growing clarity how your mind and thought forces shape your character, circumstances, and destiny.

Mind is the power that molds and makes.
And Woman is Mind, forever she takes
The tool of Thought, shaping what she wills,
Bringing forth myriad joys or countless ills.
She thinks in secret, and it comes to pass:
Her world is but her looking glass.

Thought and character are intertwined yet inseparable. A woman's thoughts shape her character, and her character influences her circumstances, which create more of the same thoughts and further mold her character. As character reveals itself through environment and circumstance, the outer conditions of a woman's life will always mirror her inner state. Her character reflects her inner world, and her thoughts reinforce that image. This doesn't mean that her circumstances at a given moment fully reflect her character, but rather, they are intimately linked to a vital thought process within her that is crucial to her growth.

Your present position is shaped by the law of your being. You are where you are today by virtue of who you are and where your thoughts have taken you. Those thoughts have molded your character and brought you to this current place in life. There's no chance element in the circumstances of your life. According to the law of cause and effect, every effect has a cause, and there is no such thing as coincidence. Everything that happens is a predictable operation of unerring natural laws. This holds true for the woman who feels "out of harmony" with her surroundings and for the woman who thrives in her environment.

You are an evolving being. Your journey on the road of life today is taking you to experiences from which you can learn and grow. As you unravel the spiritual lesson each life circumstance presents, that condition dissipates, and other circumstances arise to take its place.

As long as you believe that you are a creature of outside conditions, and that your present environment and circumstances have been shaped by those conditions, your life will be swayed by circumstances. When you understand that you have command over the hidden soil and seeds of your being, and that you are the creator of the thoughts from which your circumstances grow, you will become the rightful master of yourself and your destiny.

Circumstances spring from thought. This simple truth is well understood by those who practice any form of meditation and self-control. A woman modifies her circumstances in direct proportion to how much she changes her mindset. We can see proof of this in everyday life: when you diligently work on rectifying the flaws in your character, you will make swift and marked progress, and you'll rapidly ascend the ladder of personal growth.

The soul attracts what it needs, what it loves, what it desires, and what it fears. It can soar to the heights of its beloved aspirations or plunge to the depths of its darkest fears and desires. Circumstances are vessels through which the soul receives its own.

Every thought-seed you sow or let fall into the fertile ground of your mind, and let take root, will blossom sooner or later into action. Each seed that sprouts will bear its own fruit of opportunity and circumstance. Positive thoughts yield the sweet fruit of beneficial outcomes, and negative thoughts bear the bitter fruit of dark outcomes and regret.

The external world of circumstance molds itself to the internal world of thought. Both pleasant and undesirable external conditions contribute to a woman's ultimate good and her destiny. As the harvester of your own yield, you learn through both joy and suffering in your life.

You don't fall into adversity or stumble into trouble due to the tyranny of fate or circumstance. Instead, it happens when you tread the path of negative thoughts and base desires. A woman who nurtures positive and uplifting thoughts does not suddenly fall into a life of crime, as if suddenly thrown off course by an arbitrary external force. Her susceptibility to criminal thought was a seed planted in her mind long ago and secretly nurtured in the shadows of her heart and soul. When the moment of opportunity arrived, that seed blossomed, revealing its accumulated power.

Circumstances neither make nor
break you.
They simply reveal you to yourself.

You can't descend into vice or depravity unless those conditions reside in your mind. No such conditions can exist in your life unless your thoughts give them form. Suffering can only occur when those thoughts and resulting circumstances pull your mind into vice and negative thinking. Similarly, you can't ascend into virtue and its pure happiness without continuously sowing the seeds of virtuous aspirations. Thus, as the director of your thoughts, you are the creator of yourself, the shaper of your environment, and the author of your destiny.

Even at birth, the soul comes to its own. Through every step of its earthly pilgrimage, it attracts those conditions that reveal itself, reflecting its purity and impurity, its strength and weakness.

A woman doesn't attract what she desires but what she is. Her whims and ambitions may be frustrated at every step, but her deepest thoughts and desires are fed with their own food, be it wholesome or unhealthy, illuminated or dark, positive or negative. The "divinity that shapes our ends" is within us—it is our very self. We are only shackled by ourselves, enslaved by our own desires, weakened by our own vulnerabilities.

Thought and action are the jailers of Destiny—they confine and imprison us. Yet, thought and action are also the angels of Freedom—they liberate and inspire us to move forward in life to fulfill our spiritual destiny. We do not get what we wish and pray for, but rather, what we justly earn and deserve. Our wishes and prayers are only answered when they align with our thoughts and actions.

So, what does "fighting against circumstances" mean? It means that we are continuously rebelling against an external effect, while at the same time nurturing and holding on to the cause within ourselves. That cause could be a conscious vice or an unconscious weakness; whatever it is, it stubbornly thwarts our efforts and thus requires a remedy.

As human beings, we are eager to better our circumstances—yet, we are reluctant to better ourselves. Thus, we remain bound. If you don't shy away from hard work and you remain committed to a goal, willing to make personal sacrifices to achieve that goal, you will always accomplish what your heart is set on. This is true for both earthly and heavenly aspirations. Even a person whose sole objective in life is to gather wealth must be ready and willing to exert significant effort and make personal sacrifices to achieve that goal. A woman striving for a fulfilling and spiritually enlightened life must willing to do the same.

Consider a woman living in poverty. Wretchedly poor, she yearns to enhance her comforts and surroundings. Yet, she bemoans her circumstances, neglects her work, and believes she is justified in deceiving her employer in the belief that she is underpaid. Such a person lacks understanding of the fundamental principles that underpin true prosperity. She is not only unfit to rise out of her dire situation, but she is also attracting greater suffering by dwelling on dishonest, deceptive, and negative thoughts and by acting them out.

Imagine a wealthy woman who suffers constantly from a painful, chronic ailment brought about by over-indulgence. She's prepared to spend vast sums of money to alleviate the disease, yet she refuses to curb her indulgent desires. She wishes to satisfy her cravings for unhealthy foods while also enjoying good health. Such a woman will not achieve good health, because she has not yet learned the basic principles of a healthy and balanced lifestyle.

Imagine a woman in business who resorts to underhanded tactics to evade taxes, and she cuts her employees' salaries in a bid to boost profits. Such a person is unfit for prosperity. She hasn't yet grasped the fundamental principles of fair play and generosity. When she finds herself bankrupt, both in reputation and riches, she blames others for her misfortune, or she attributes it to "bad luck," not realizing that she is the architect of her misfortune. Her failure is a direct result of her thoughts and the actions they inspired.

These examples illustrate the often unconscious yet indisputable fact: you are the driver on your life journey and the architect of your own circumstances. While you may strive for positive goals, you simultaneously thwart your own success by fostering thoughts and desires that are in direct conflict with your goals. If you expect success but harbor thoughts of failure and act in ways that affirm these thoughts, you make failure a self-fulfilling prophecy.

Observing others in everyday life can provide valuable insights into how you can be the maker of your own circumstances, both good and bad. But the most profound understanding comes from introspective reflection on your own thoughts and actions. Without such introspection, merely reading about these concepts is unlikely to inspire change or bring you closer to realizing your goals and destiny.

In the intricate tapestry of life, the threads that depict your circumstances may be so entangled, your thoughts so deeply ingrained, or your vision of happiness so far from your present reality that an outsider cannot discern the state of your spirit by observing your outer life. A woman's experiences and emotions are complex and personal, and the assumptions of an outsider often miss the truth.

Consider two women—one appears honest yet faces constant adversity, while the other appears dishonest, yet she thrives. Those who misunderstand the workings of thought might conclude that the first woman fails due to her honesty, while the second prospers because of her dishonesty. These assumptions view the world through a black-and-white lens and oversimplify the nuances of human character. They imagine the dishonest woman as almost totally corrupt, and the honest one as purely virtuous. But reality is never that clear cut. The dishonest woman may possess virtues that the honest one lacks, and the honest woman may harbor flaws absent in the other. Every woman reaps the outcomes of her actions and thoughts—both the good and the bad.

It's an all-too-human tendency to believe that a kind, honest, and optimistic woman suffers because of her virtues. Those who misunderstand the natural laws of thought might see virtues as weaknesses and assume that a virtuous woman who suffers defeat lacks ambition or persistence. Yet, it's an oversimplification to attribute our sufferings to our good qualities and not our flaws. Only when we have purged every negative thought from our minds and cleared every shadow from our souls can we truly say this. As we journey towards this state of spiritual clarity, we'll come to realize that the universe operates in a just and unerring order—we can't harvest good from evil or evil from good. With this understanding, we'll look back at our past misjudgments, knowing that our life is, and always has been, justly arranged. We'll recognize all past experiences, pleasant and unpleasant, as the fair outcomes of our evolving yet imperfect selves.

Positive thoughts and actions cannot yield negative outcomes. Negative thoughts and actions cannot produce positive results. You reap what you sow—corn seeds will only sprout corn, and nettles will only give rise to more nettles. Many women grasp this principle in nature and work in harmony with it. However, few recognize its relevance to morality, even though it works just as plainly and predictably there. Hence, they miss the opportunity to align with it.

Suffering is always a sign that your thoughts have veered off course, causing you to live out of sync with yourself and the laws of your existence. It serves to purge and refine you, burning away what is useless and flawed and nudging us along the path from imperfection to supreme perfection. When you've achieved purity and balance and understanding, you will no longer suffer.

The circumstances in a woman's life that cause her distress are rooted in disordered and negative thoughts. Conversely, the circumstances that bring her joy and peace stem from harmonious and positive thoughts. Such blessings are the fruit of right thoughts and right actions. Misery, not poverty or lack of wealth, is the true reflection of wrong thought. A woman can be wealthy yet tormented, or she can be content despite her poverty. True bliss and riches only come together when wealth is used wisely and correctly. A woman in poverty only sinks into misery when she believes her condition is unjustly imposed.

Extreme poverty and excess—two sides of the same coin—both stem from unhealthy thinking. Conversely, happiness, health, and prosperity naturally arise from an inner-outer balance and harmony with one's surroundings.

Life only begins when you stop wallowing, complaining, and harboring resentment, and start searching for the hidden justice that regulates all life. As you align your mind with this guiding principle, you stop blaming others for your condition and instead strengthen yourself with noble and resilient thoughts. You cease to resist circumstances but instead start leveraging them as catalysts for progress, discovering your latent abilities and potential.

Order, not chaos, is the governing principle of the Universe. Justice, not injustice, is the soul and substance of life. Integrity, not corruption, is the empowering force in the spiritual governance of the world. Understanding this, you'll see that by setting your own life straight, you align with the Universe. During this transformative process, you'll find that as you change your thoughts towards things and other people, they in turn will change towards you.

Through diligent self-reflection and introspection, you can confirm that your thoughts and desires shape your circumstances, and your circumstances reinforce your thoughts and desires. If you make significant changes in your thoughts, you will be astonished and gratified at the swift transformation it brings about in your life.

Many people deceive themselves, believing they can secretly harbor dark and depraved thoughts without them coming to light. They cannot. Such thoughts quickly manifest as desires, which soon crystallize into habits. These habits harden into sensation-seeking and addiction, which spiral into conditions of degradation and poverty. Unhealthy thoughts crystallize into disordered and disabling habits, leading to circumstances of discord and disease. Thoughts of fear, doubt, and indecision crystallize into weak and irresolute habits, which harden into circumstances of failure, dependence, and poverty.

Similarly, idle and unfocused thoughts crystallize into habits of apathy and pessimism, which harden into situations of despair and defeat. Hateful and judgmental thoughts crystallize into habits of accusation and violence, which harden into circumstances of persecution and cruelty. Selfish thoughts of all kinds crystallize into habits of self-seeking and greed, leading to situations of deprivation and loss, wherein the more we seek, the more we lose, and what we most desire in life is taken away.

On the other hand, beautiful thoughts crystallize into habits of optimism, honesty, and compassion, which solidify into bright and sunny circumstances. Wholesome thoughts crystallize into habits of temperance and self-control, leading to situations of balance and peace. Thoughts of courage, confidence, and self-reliance crystallize into noble habits, resulting in circumstances of freedom and success.

Likewise, energetic and motivated thoughts crystallize into habits of hard work and accomplishment, which solidify into prosperity and attainment. Gentle, forgiving thoughts crystallize into habits of kindness and empathy, which solidify into secure and harmonious circumstances. Loving and unselfish thoughts crystallize into habits of affection and generosity, resulting in situations of divine love and spiritual enlightenment.

Any train of thought that you persist in—whether good or bad—will have a distinct and noticeable effect on your character, which in turn will shape your circumstances. While you cannot directly control your circumstances in life, you can choose your thoughts, whether those thoughts serve to motivate action or precipitate reaction, and in doing so, indirectly yet surely shape your circumstances.

The natural law of cause and effect means that the thoughts you dwell upon will materialize in your life. Life will present you with opportunities that will swiftly bring both your good and bad thoughts to the surface, then reward them accordingly.

If you give up destructive and vengeful thoughts, the world will soften towards you and be ready to help you. If you give up weak and pessimistic thoughts, you will see opportunities spring up all around to reward your newfound outlook. Nurture positive thoughts, and you will never be shackled by despair or shame—your future will shine with happiness, success, and peace, rewarding your efforts justly.

The world is your kaleidoscope, and the ever-shifting colors it displays from moment to moment are the beautifully synchronized reflections of your ever-evolving thoughts. As your thoughts shift and evolve, what you attract will change. What you see around you will change. Your surroundings will transform, and your life conditions will adjust, for better or worse, reflecting your evolving mindset.

> *You shall become what you choose to be.*
> *Let failure find its false content.*
> *In the circumstances of your environment*
> *Your spirit yearns to be free.*
> *It masters time, it conquers space;*
> *It quiets the boastful trickster Chance,*

> *And dethrones the tyrant Circumstance,*
> *To relegate it to a servant's place.*
> *The human Will, that unseen force,*
> *Born from the soul, which never dies,*
> *Can carve a path to any prize.*
> *Be not hasty to delay,*
> *But wait as one who understands;*
> *When spirit rises and commands,*
> *The universe stands ready to obey.*

Further Insights

In this chapter, we examined the power of the mind, using the metaphor of a fertile garden to symbolize our mental landscapes, and where our thoughts represent the seeds that we plant. We learned that a direct correlation exists between the quality of our thoughts and the quality of our lives. As women, we understand the importance of kind and nurturing thoughts. Positive thoughts are likened to planting sweet corn, a source of nourishment, while planting negative thought-seeds is akin to sowing nettles, which sting and cause discomfort. By consciously cultivating empowering thoughts and removing negativity, we have the ability to shape our life path and destiny, for better or worse.

The lesson conveyed in this chapter is clear, but it can be easily obscured by the chaos and distractions of daily life. To truly experience joy, fulfillment, and success, we must not allow the nettles of negativity to take root in our minds. We must recognize that our thoughts have the power to manifest into positive actions and outcomes, but only if we consciously cultivate empowering thoughts and diligently weed out the negative ones that cause disruption and trigger destructive cycles in our lives.

The concept of "We reap what we sow" resonates as a universal law found in various philosophies and religions. It reflects the idea of cause and effect, or Karma, which governs our physical world as well as our spiritual existence. Every action and thought we have will trigger a corresponding reaction or outcome. The seeds we sow in the garden of our mind bear the fruit of our nurtured thoughts.

This chapter also underscores the inseparability of thought and character. Our thoughts shape our character, and our character, in turn, attracts circumstances that reinforce those thoughts, creating a continuous cycle. We have the choice of whether this cycle leads us into a downward spiral of negativity or uplifts us towards positivity. The decision is ours to make.

It's important to note that the terms "positive" and "negative," "good" and "bad," are used here and throughout this book in a philosophical context and without moral judgment. What is considered "good" can vary from person to person, and may even change for an individual based on their life's conditions, health, emotions, and spiritual state at a given time.

As a woman, you possess the inner strength and resilience to navigate the highs and lows of life. Take a moment to reflect on your life journey in recent months. Try to identify the cause-and-effect relationships between your thoughts, actions, and the circumstances in your life. Are your thoughts and actions nurturing success or breeding disappointment? Use these insights to assess your current situation. Are you consciously cultivating a positive mindset and taking steps that carve a path towards success and fulfillment?

Ultimately, you hold the power to shape your life and destiny, one thought at a time. Your experiences as a woman offer unique perspectives and valuable insights. Use them to cultivate a thriving landscape in the garden of your life.

Chapter 3

How Thought Affects Health and Body

The body is a reflection of a woman's mind. It mirrors her thoughts and obeys her mind's directives, whether consciously chosen or unconsciously expressed. As a restless sea reflects a tempestuous sky, a woman's body reflects the turbulence of her thoughts. When her mind swirls with negative, angry, or destructive thoughts, her body can become a canvas of disease and decay. The more she entangles herself in these negative thoughts, the stronger their impact and the deeper her health sinks into the mire. Conversely, when her mind is a serene sky of positive, beautiful thoughts, her body radiates with vitality and grace, as peaceful waters reflect a clear, bright sky.

Health and disease, like circumstances, are fruits born from the tree of thought. Unhealthy thoughts—anger, fear, hatred, jealousy, obsession, and others—are the seeds that can undermine your physical health. Thoughts of fear and despair can shorten or extinguish life as swiftly as a bullet, and these negative thoughts are draining the vitality from millions of women today.

Those who allow fear of disease to preoccupy their thoughts become more susceptible to it. Anxiety weakens the body, making it more vulnerable to disease. Even negative thoughts that aren't physically acted upon can overload and damage the nervous system.

In contrast, strong, pure, and joyful thoughts strengthen the body and act as a protective shield, promoting vitality, wellness, and a healthy constitution. The body is a delicate and responsive instrument; it dances to the music composed and played by the mind. Habits of thought will leave their imprint on the body, for better or worse.

As long as a woman weaves negative, destructive, and unevolved thoughts, she will continue to be troubled by disease and physical ailments. As long as she clings to base and unhealthy desires, she will suffer addictions and their detrimental effects on her body, mind, and soul. Out of a defiled mind sprouts a defiled life and a corrupt body. Conversely, from a clean heart grows a wholesome life and a clean body. Thought is the architect of all actions, and the results of those actions construct our circumstances. Make the fountain pure and all that a woman is and aspires will follow with beauty and harmony.

A change of diet will not help a woman who will not change her thoughts. As a river cannot be redirected without altering its source, a woman cannot change her physical habits without first changing her mental habits. When a woman balances and immerses her thoughts in a positive mindset, her body and mind find harmony, and she no longer craves food or overeats. Clean thoughts blossom and give form to clean habits. Clean habits bring forth and nourish a healthy body and a vibrant spirit. The woman who has fortified and purified her thoughts stands above the fear of disease.

Just as a woman protects her body, she must guard her mind. As she would protect her hands while using a sharp knife, she must shield her mind from idle and negative thoughts. Nurture the body, beautify the mind. Exercise the body in healthy ways, and similarly, engage the mind in healthy discourse. Purify the mind, and you dispel emotional unease; cleanse the emotions, and you banish disease from the body.

Thoughts of malice, jealousy, depression, and failure drain the life force from the body, leaving it depleted and rendering an individual sickly, prone to aches and pains, and exhausted. A gloomy countenance does not materialize in a woman by chance—it is sculpted by gloomy thoughts. Wrinkles etched on a woman's face are the fingerprints left by folly, passion, and fear in the garden of her mind and soul.

I know a woman of ninety-six years who has the bright, innocent face of a girl. I know a man who is barely thirty, yet his face is etched with harsh lines, making him appear much older and weary. The woman's visage is the result of a sweet and sunny disposition; the man's, a reflection of turbulent passions and discontent.

To have a sweet and wholesome home, you must open the windows to admit fresh air and invite the sunshine into your rooms. Similarly, a healthy body and a radiant, joyful countenance can only be achieved by opening the windows of the mind and letting in thoughts of joy and goodwill, and seeking tranquility.

As a woman matures, her face becomes a canvas upon which the brushstrokes of her life experience are etched. On one woman, we see wrinkles imprinted by compassion and sympathy. On another, we see faint lines drawn by strong, pure, and joyful thoughts. On yet another, we see deep furrows carved by unrestrained passions. We can easily distinguish one from the other. Those who have weathered storms of stress, unbridled passion, and anger bear intense emotions etched in the lines of their faces. For those who have walked paths of kindness, compassion, and peace, age manifests as a calm, soft glow, like the gentle setting sun.

There is no physician more potent than bright and cheerful thought for dissipating the ills and impurities of the body. There is no comforter greater than goodwill for dispersing the clouds of anger, grief, and sorrow. To live perpetually in thoughts of ill-will, greed, envy, and fear is to be confined in a self-made prison. But to think well of all, to be cheerful with all, to learn to find the good in all—these benevolent and unselfish thoughts are the very gateways to heaven.

To dwell day by day in thoughts of love and peace towards every person and creature we encounter is to invite abounding joy and peace into our lives. Such are the rewards and the supreme good fortune of the woman who nurtures these thoughts.

Further Insights

This chapter sheds light on the power that your mind can have over your body, and it illustrates how your thoughts can significantly impact your physical health. It uses the metaphor of a woman's body being a canvas that reflects the colors of her thoughts. If her mind is filled with dark and destructive thoughts, her body becomes vulnerable to the effects of that negativity and can manifest signs of disease and decay. In contrast, when her mind is a serene landscape of positivity, her body radiates vitality and beauty.

This relationship between thoughts and health is not merely a fad notion but has been confirmed by science. Medical experts and researchers have established that an individual's mental state can influence their physical health in profound ways. Just a few of the healthful benefits of positive thinking include lower levels of stress, a longer life span, increased resistance to common illnesses like the cold, and even a reduced risk of severe diseases such as cardiovascular disorders.

Consider a study of 604 hospital patients in Denmark, published in *JAMA Psychiatry*. It found that found that people with pessimistic views are 55% more likely to die in the next decade, and men with pessimistic outlooks were much more likely to die early. The study also reported that those who cultivated a positive outlook were 58% more likely to live at least another five years. Thus, having an optimistic outlook could significantly boost your longevity.

Dr. Suzanne Segerstrom, a psychology professor at the University of Kentucky, undertook a study of 124 freshman law students, and she corroborated the mind-body connection and a clear nexus between optimism and a healthy immune system. Her research found that those who fostered a positive mindset had robust immunity, while those with a pessimistic outlook had a weakened immune response and were more susceptible to illness. This finding underscores an irony that those who harbor a fear of falling ill are often the ones who end up doing so.

In a study published in *Circulation*, a journal of the American Heart Association, researchers found a link between a positive outlook and heart health. Optimistic individuals were less prone to developing coronary heart disease compared to their pessimistic counterparts. Another study found that people with higher levels of optimism had a 73% lower risk of heart failure compared with pessimistic individuals. And a study published in the *Canadian Medical Association Journal* reported that adults over the age of 60 who indulged in negative thinking were more likely to experience health problems and mobility issues. In contrast, their optimistic counterparts fared better in maintaining their mobility and overall health.

Given these facts, it is clear that the power of the mind over the body is not just a vague concept or cliché but a tangible reality with real-world implications. The negative thoughts you harbor may be more than just mentally draining—they could also be damaging your health and shortening your lifespan. Conversely, positive thinking can act as a protective shield, enhancing your health, slowing down aging, and contributing to a longer, more vibrant life.

As a woman, you may face numerous challenges and stressors in day-to-day living, but remember, your thoughts hold immense power. They can lead you to a path of vitality and wellness, or one of disease and decay. Harness this power to build a mindset of positivity. Doing so will not only uplift your spirit but also lead to better health and a longer, more fulfilling life.

Chapter 4

A Woman's Thoughts and Purpose

Thought is futile and has no power unless it shaped and driven by purpose. Without purpose, thought is wasted, a rudderless ship adrift in the sea, its energy squandered and its potential unrealized. Until thought is harnessed to a purpose, there can be no intelligent accomplishment. It's akin to scattering seeds haphazardly, hoping that they will take root and flourish. But more often than not, those seeds are tossed into the wind and lost, their potential for growth denied. A woman must be like a skilled gardener, planting her seeds of thought with intention, nurturing them, and guiding their growth towards a clear goal.

Time is precious, and the present moment is a fleeting gift that should be cherished and utilized effectively. Each day should be an opportunity to progress towards happiness, fulfillment, and the realization of one's spiritual destiny.

Those without a purpose in life readily succumb to negative emotions. Anxiety, fear, resentment, self-doubt, and similar emotions are indications of weakness and will lead to unhappiness and failure, just as surely as if you had set out to achieve those outcomes. In this ever-evolving universe teeming with potential, there is no place for procrastination or weakness. It is crucial to conceive a purpose, a goal that resonates with your heart and mind. Let this goal be the lighthouse that guides your thoughts and actions. Make this purpose the focal point of your thoughts. Whether it's a spiritual ideal or a worldly ambition, focus your energy on achieving it. Make this purpose your highest duty and dedicate yourself to it every day. Do not let your thoughts wander to the distractions of aimless daydreaming and wishful thinking. This is the key to mastering self-control and harnessing the true power of focused thought.

The path to your goal may be challenging, and you may stumble and fall numerous times before you succeed. But it is in these trials that you develop courage and determination. Each failure, each setback is a stepping-stone towards greater strength and wisdom, setting the stage for future victories.

If you feel daunted by the idea of a grand purpose, start with perfecting the small tasks of everyday life. As you become proficient in these seemingly trivial activities, you will gain confidence, and your greater purpose will come into focus. Once this happens, no goal will be too lofty, no dream too big. Everything that you can imagine will be within the realm of possibility and what you can accomplish.

Even the weakest soul, once it recognizes its frailty and understands that strength can only come from sincere effort and practice, can grow strong. It's a journey of persistence and patience, of adding strength upon strength, until the soul evolves into an infinite source of power.

Just as a woman can transform physical weakness into strength through consistent training and a diligent exercise regimen, so too she can transform her weak thoughts into powerful ones through willpower and the practice of positive thinking.

To begin thinking with purpose, you must first let go of laziness and muster the strength to overcome mental weakness and unhealthy habits that can impact both body and mind. This is the passport to the realm of the strong and the determined, those who view failure not as a dead-end but merely a detour or delay on the road to success. A strong woman makes her circumstances serve her purpose. She thinks powerfully, acts fearlessly, and executes efficiently.

Having defined your goal or purpose, chart a straight course towards its achievement. Begin now, without delay or procrastination, and stay the course, undeterred by distractions or obstacles. Set aside doubt and fear—they are the adversaries of progress; they scatter your efforts and render them ineffectual. The seeds of accomplishment—purpose, energy, and the will to achieve—wither and die in the face of doubt and fear.

The genesis of achievement lies in holding a firm belief in our capabilities, in our competence, in our ability to overcome obstacles and adversity, and in our potential to succeed. A woman's belief in her abilities is the foundation of her will to achieve. She must understand that success springs from the knowledge that she can succeed.

Doubt and fear are the twin saboteurs of success. The woman who allows these destructive weeds to sprout and grow in the garden of her mind sabotages her journey towards her goals. She may find herself trapped in a self-fulfilling cycle of failure, where her fears or worries dictate her actions, or more often, her inaction. This destructive synergy is evident in thoughts like, "I'd love to start a business, but what if it fails? Maybe I should stay in my current job, even though I'm unhappy." Or "I'd love to apply for that leadership position, but what if I am not good enough? Maybe I should wait until I have more experience." The unfortunate result is that she doesn't pursue the things that she knows are important to her, and her potential remains untapped.

Conquer doubt and fear, and you will conquer failure. With this victory, every thought you nurture will be allied with the force of your will and the power to succeed. Every challenge you face will be met with courage; every obstacle and setback will be overcome. Your ambitions, the seeds sown in the garden of your mind, will blossom in their appropriate season and be cultivated in their own time, bearing fruit that does not fall prematurely but ripens fully in its own time.

Thought allied to purpose becomes a creative force. Grasp this concept and you will find yourself poised on the threshold of transformation, ready to evolve into more than just a jumble of wavering thoughts and shifting sensations. You will become the conscious, intelligent wielder of your mental powers, asserting your rightful authority as the master gardener of your mind and architect of your destiny, purposefully tending to your thoughts as they grow into the realities of your life.

Further Insights

This chapter explores the nexus between positive thought, our intentions, and our life goals. It reminds us that lack of purpose in daily life can cause a woman to drift into the labyrinth of negative emotions, such as anxiety, self-doubt, fear, and a sense of futility. A woman with no goals or purpose has nothing to fill her time but dwelling on that unfortunate belief—she has no goal or purpose. As she sinks deeper into the hopelessness and futility of her life, her thoughts lead her deeper into the quicksand of despair.

We can conceptualize a life without purpose as a sailboat adrift on the ocean, devoid of a rudder and sail. It bobs aimlessly from wave to wave, tossed about by the whims of the wind, making random turns leading nowhere. Inevitably, the sailor caught in this aimless drift may find herself swallowed by a tempest, her life squandered and her potential unrealized.

The absence of a purpose at a particular moment

should not be a cause for despair. It is a temporary phase, a brief pause in the symphony of life. During such times, focus your thoughts on the mundane tasks of everyday living to keep your mind active and your spirit strong, so that when the grand adventure of life reveals itself, you are ready to seize it.

As this chapter explains, those who are yet to discover a grand purpose to their lives should channel their energies towards the flawless execution of everyday tasks. Such focus is necessary to cultivate determination, motivation, and mental energy. Once this is achieved, every goal you can imagine becomes a tangible reality that can be grasped and realized.

It's natural to feel a sense of awe and even envy when hearing tales of women who discovered their calling in childhood, or those who suddenly one day had an epiphany about their life's mission. You might find yourself wondering, "Why haven't I experienced a profound revelation? Does my life lack purpose?"

Realize that such bursts of sudden enlightenment are more the exception than the norm. Most people do not experience an electrifying awakening of purpose. Instead, your sense of direction might be a gentle whisper rather than a thunderous epiphany, subtly guiding you towards your destiny.

Also remember that your life purpose may evolve and change as you progress toward your destiny. A goal that enthralled you as a youth may lose its charm or appeal as you mature. And that's perfectly okay. Purpose isn't a static concept—it's a dynamic process that ebbs and flows with the tide of life.

Consider Anna Mary Robertson Moses, affectionately known as Grandma Moses. She discovered her passion for painting at the ripe age of seventy-eight and became a globally acclaimed American folk artist. Her paintings not only adorned prestigious museums but also brought joy to countless people through heartwarming greeting cards. Her masterpiece, *The Sugaring Off,* fetched an impressive US$1.2 million in 2006. Her journey is a testament to the fact that it's never too late to discover your purpose, and age is just a number when it comes to pursuing your dreams.

Inspiration is the magical catalyst that reveals your life purpose and propels you towards your destiny. An idea that sparks a flame in your heart today could evolve into a significant goal or even your greatest achievement in the future. To unearth your purpose, irrespective of your age or stage in life, you must attune yourself to the whispers of your inner voice. Keep your mind unburdened by fear, doubt, and depression to clearly hear the soft, sweet symphony of your soul. Only then will you be ready to fully embrace the magnificent journey of a purposeful life.

Chapter 5

Thought and the Pathway to Achievement

*A*ll that we achieve or fail to achieve is the direct result of our own thoughts. Thus, our pathway in life is formed and directed by the power of our thoughts.

The Universe is governed by order and natural laws. Toss an apple in the air, and it falls back to the ground due to the law of gravity. Similarly, loss of self-control and equilibrium open the door to chaos and destruction. The choices we make on our life journey are wholly ours. We cannot blame others for the path we walk when it is the path of our own choosing.

As a woman, you are the architect of your life, its joys and sorrows, its triumphs and trials—all are the consequences of your choices. You are the dreamer of your dreams, the maker of your destiny. All that befalls you along the way is the reward or consequence of your free will.

The virtues and vulnerabilities that shape your character, the dreams that inspire you, and the fears that unsettle you—all are products of your thought processes. Your talents and faults, your hopes and fears, are yours and yours alone. They are the seeds you have planted in your mind as time has gone by. Only you can transform them. Only you can water the seeds that will blossom into exquisite flowers, and remove the weeds hindering their growth. Likewise, the circumstances of your life are creations of your own thought processes, not mere results of luck or happenstance. Joy and suffering are born from within.

> *As you think, so you are.*
> *As you continue to think*
> *in the same manner,*
> *so you remain.*

Just as you are a reflection of your thoughts, so your reflection remains unchanged and becomes even more entrenched as you persist in those thoughts.

Imagine a strong and compassionate woman on her life's journey pausing to help another who is struggling. She knows in her heart that it's the compassionate thing to do. But she also understands that a strong person cannot help a weaker one unless that individual is willing to be helped, and willing to help herself. To truly rise, the woman in need must find strength within herself, the kind of strength she admires in her benefactor. She must learn to become strong herself. Ultimately, no one but she can alter her circumstances or cultivate her inner strength.

Conventional wisdom leads us to believe that the oppressed are victims of the oppressor, so it's easy to despise the oppressor. Some argue that the oppressor exists only because weaker individuals are willing to be oppressed, thus shifting blame onto the oppressed. Both perspectives miss the truth of the matter. The oppressor and the oppressed are both trapped in a cycle of ignorance, partners in this mournful dance. It may seem like one inflicts suffering onto the other, but in reality, they both torment themselves. A profound understanding is required to recognize the law at work in the weakness of the oppressed and the oppressor's misuse of power. A perfect Love sees the pain inherent in both conditions and does not judge. A perfect Compassion extends to both the oppressor and the oppressed, understanding that they are entwined in each other's suffering.

A woman who has overcome her weakness and can no longer be subjugated, as well as a woman who has discarded her selfish thoughts and no longer seeks to subjugate others, are neither the oppressor nor the oppressed. They are free.

You can only rise up and achieve by lifting up your thoughts. You can only remain weak, abject, and miserable by refusing to lift up your thoughts. Your ascent, your victories, your accomplishments are all guided by the uplifting of your thoughts. If you resist this upliftment, you will remain weak, disheartened, and unhappy.

Before you can achieve anything, even simple objectives, you must elevate your thoughts beyond the shadows of doubt and fear. To attain success, you must rid yourself of resentment, impulsiveness, and other negative emotions. These disruptive thought-seeds, at the very least, will divert you from your goal; at worst, they will undermine your efforts and bring certain failure.

It is not necessary to completely give up all selfish desires and impulsive tendencies to achieve success, but you must be willing to sacrifice a portion of them. If your senses are clouded by doubts or indulgent habits, your thinking will lack clarity, your planning will lack method. This clouded thinking will prevent you from discovering and cultivating the skills and talents necessary to reach your goal. Without control over your thoughts, you'll struggle to manage external events or shoulder serious responsibilities. Independent action and self-reliance will be out of reach.

The path to progress is paved with sacrifice. Your success will be directly proportional to the extent you can let go of your base desires and focus your mind on realizing your plans. Your success will also hinge on your ability to redirect the energy you've been wasting on unhealthy thoughts and habits towards strengthening your resolve and self-reliance. The higher you lift your thoughts, the wiser you become. The wiser you are, the greater your success and the more lasting your achievements will be.

The Universe does not favor those who are cruel, greedy, dishonest, depraved, or those who dwell in the dark shadows of their souls. The Law of Karma, or cause and effect, may seem to work in unpredictable ways, leading some people to mistakenly believe that ours is a chaotic world where the good are punished and the evil rewarded. In reality, the Universe favors those who are generous, honest, gentle, and virtuous. This is a truth that has been echoed by great Teachers throughout the ages in various forms. To understand this, confirm it, and manifest it in your life, you need to persist in making yourself more positive and virtuous, and you do that by uplifting your thoughts.

Intellectual achievements result from thoughts devoted to the pursuit of knowledge or the search for beauty and truth in life and nature. While these accomplishments may sometimes be motivated by vanity or ambition, their true source is consistent effort and pure, unselfish thoughts.

Spiritual achievements are the culmination of divine aspirations. If your thoughts are lofty and spiritual, and your mind is focused on all that is positive and unselfish, then, as surely as the sun reaches its zenith and the moon waxes full, you will become wise and virtuous in character. A woman who becomes wise and virtuous will ascend to a position of influence and blessedness.

Achievement, regardless of its nature, is the result of effort and the ultimate aim of thought. By diligently practicing self-control and directing thought wisely, a woman can reach the pinnacle of success. Or, by choosing the weaker path and succumbing to sensuality, laziness, corruption, and confusion, she may descend into the dark abyss of despair and failure.

It is possible to achieve great success in the world and attain lofty heights in your spiritual journey, only to descend back into weakness and failure by allowing arrogant, selfish, and corrupt thoughts to take root in the garden of your mind. The victories achieved by right thought can only be maintained by watchful vigilance. Some women, upon achieving success, relax their guard, falling back into old habits and negative thought patterns, and they swiftly descend back into despair and failure.

Every achievement, whether moral, intellectual, or material, is the result of directed thought. Your accomplishments, as well as your failures, are governed by the same law and are achieved through the same method—the only difference lies in the goal you pursue or the object of your attainment.

A woman who seeks modest achievements must be prepared to make modest sacrifices. A woman who aspires to achieve much should be willing to sacrifice much. But a woman who aims for the greatest and loftiest goals must be prepared to make the greatest of sacrifices.

Further Insights

This chapter examines how thoughts ultimately crystallize into actions and serve as the bedrock for success or failure. The concept that positive thoughts act as a magnet for success and abundance is a theme often repeated in the writings of James Allen, and it echoes across many religious and philosophical teachings dating back to antiquity. For instance, the Taoist scriptures provide insight into this concept, stating: "Those who are thus, are good: people honor them; Heaven's Reason gives them grace. Blessings and abundance follow them. Bad luck keeps away; angel spirits guard them. Whatever they undertake will surely succeed, and even to spiritual saintliness they may aspire." The term "Heaven's Reason" refers to the natural order or universal moral law.

In keeping with this idea, let's consider the wisdom found in the Buddhist text, *The Dhammapada*, which likely was a source of inspiration for James Allen in his books. This ancient text provides an invaluable roadmap of guidance, with teachings that encourage mindfulness, self-control, truth-seeking, and a focus on good deeds, while warning against impulsiveness, indulgence, and a preoccupation with negative thoughts and actions.

1. All that we are is the result of what we have thought: it is founded on our thoughts; it is made up of our thoughts. If a man speaks or acts with an evil thought, pain follows him, as the wheel follows the foot of the ox that draws the carriage.

2. All that we are is the result of what we have thought: it is founded on our thoughts; it is made up of our thoughts. If a man speaks or acts with a pure thought, happiness follows him, like a shadow that never leaves him.

3. "He abused me, he beat me, he defeated me, he robbed me..." In those who harbor such thoughts, hatred will never cease.

4. "He abused me, he beat me, he defeated me, he robbed me..." In those who do not harbor such thoughts, hatred will cease.

5. For hatred does not cease by hatred in any situation: hatred ceases by love. This is the age-old rule.

6. The world does not know that we must all come to an end here. But those who know it, their quarrels cease at once.

7. He who lives looking for pleasures only, his senses uncontrolled, immoderate in his food, idle, and weak, Mâra (The Temptress) will certainly overthrow him, as the wind throws down a weak tree.

8. He who lives without looking for pleasures, his senses well-controlled, moderate in his food, faithful and strong, Mâra will certainly not overthrow him, any more than the wind throws down a rocky mountain.

9. He who wishes to wear the yellow robe (of the priest) without having cleansed himself of sin, who disregards temperance and truth, is unworthy of the yellow robe.

10. But he who has cleansed himself of sin, who is well grounded in all virtues, and follows temperance and truth, he is indeed worthy of the yellow robe.

11. They who imagine truth in untruth, and see untruth in truth, never arrive at truth but follow vain desires.

12. They who know truth in truth, and untruth in untruth, arrive at truth and follow true desires.

13. As rain breaks through a house with an unsound roof, passion will break through an unreflecting mind.

14. As rain does not break through a well-roofed house, passion will not break through a well-reflecting mind.

15. The evil-doer mourns in this world, and he mourns in the next; he mourns in both. He mourns and suffers when he sees the evil of his own work.

16. The virtuous man delights in this world, and he delights in the next—he delights in both. He delights and rejoices when he sees the purity of his own work.

17. The evil-doer suffers in this world, and he suffers in the next; he suffers in both. He suffers when he thinks of the evil he has done; he suffers more when traveling on the evil path.

18. The virtuous man is happy in this world, and he is happy in the next; he is happy in both. He is happy when he thinks of the good he has done; he is even happier when traveling on the good path.

19. The thoughtless man, even if he can recite a large portion of the law but does not practice it, has no share in the spiritual quest; he is like a cow herder counting the cows of others.

20. The follower of the law, even if he can recite only a small portion of it but has forsaken passion,

hatred, and foolishness, possesses true knowledge and serenity of mind. Caring for nothing in this world or what is to come, he has a share in the spiritual quest.

Despite such profound wisdom being readily available in our modern world, many women struggle with the mundane challenges of daily living. They find themselves tossed about on the turbulent sea of life, often losing direction amidst the shifting tides of pessimism, fear, and self-doubt all around them.

Humans are quick learners. We absorb lessons from experiences and pass the torch of knowledge in science, history, and culture from one generation to the next. Yet, in our personal lives, we often overlook the wisdom offered by others, choosing to learn the hard way. We can be told that touching a hot stove will burn, yet some of us must feel the burn ourselves to believe it or truly understand.

Reflect on a situation when a trusted friend or loved one suggested that you take a particular course of action based on their experiences. Did you heed the advice, or did you choose to navigate your own path, only to regret your decision later? Ponder those experiences, and consider how being more receptive to the wisdom of others may be beneficial. Realize that people with greater wisdom have managed to chart their journey through life, and their experiences may serve as guiding lights in your life. We can learn much from the experiences of others. Their insights can help us avoid suffering and failure, and chart our way to a more fulfilling life and spiritual destiny.

In the face of societal pressures and expectations, it's especially crucial for women to harness the power of positive thinking and mindful action. By incorporating this wisdom into daily living, a woman can become the master-gardener of her soul, shaping her circumstances and outcomes, and cultivating an environment of success and abundance. This realization is a powerful tool that she can use to transform her life, reinforcing the truth that thoughts do indeed shape reality.

Take a moment today to reflect on your thoughts. Are they serving you, or are they holding you back? Remember, you have the power to shape your reality.

Chapter 6

Dreams, Visions, and Ideals

*D*reamers are the lifelines of humanity. They are the prophets who glimpse the future; the prodigies whose intellect and creativity enrich society; the messengers who guide humanity on its path to enlightenment. Just as the visible world is underpinned by the invisible, humanity, through its trials, transgressions, and mundane fascinations, draws sustenance from the beautiful visions of its solitary dreamers.

Humanity cannot forget its dreamers, nor let their visions and ideals fade into oblivion. We live through them, finding them in realities that have yet to materialize. Artists, poets, composers, sculptors, authors, prophets—these are the weavers of our world and the builders of our path to the Divine. The world is a more beautiful place because they have lived. Without them, toiling humanity would wilt and fade.

Nurture a beautiful vision, a dream in your heart, and one day it will be your reality. Marie Curie followed her dream of achieving scientific breakthroughs, and she transformed the landscape of medicine, earning a Nobel prize in physics. Columbus dreamt of unexplored lands, and he discovered them. Susan B. Anthony envisioned a world where women and African American slaves had equal rights with men, and she paved the way to the dawn of an era of greater equality. Buddha saw a vision of a spiritual realm of unparalleled beauty and perfect peace, and he entered it.

Embrace your visions. Hold on to your ideals. Cherish the music that plays in your heart, the art that colors your mind, the words of stories that come alive in your imagination. Treasure the beauty that takes shape in your mind's eye, and the joy that radiates from your purest thoughts. Out of these will grow all delightful conditions. Stay true to them, and your perfect world will be built.

To desire is to obtain; to aspire is to achieve. There is a subtle difference between the two that the spiritually awakened woman understands. Desire motivates us to obtain material possessions; aspiration propels us towards noble goals. Should a woman's superficial desires be fully gratified, while her purest aspirations starve for lack of nourishment? Material wealth is fleeting and elusive, crumbling and fading into nothing. Every material object around you will eventually disintegrate. But the soul is eternal, transcending this temporal world to merge with the endless, everlasting universe.

Become the woman who is respected and adored by all others. Strive to realize your loftiest goals. Aspire to make your dreams come true. Reach further and higher than those who are content with mundane labors that are performed without thanks. "Ask and it will be given," and your aspirations will materialize.

Dream grand dreams. As you dream, so shall you become. Your Vision is the promise of what you shall one day be. Your Ideal is the prophecy of what you will reveal.

The greatest achievements were at first and for a time dreams. The oak sleeps in the acorn; the bird waits in the egg. In the highest vision of the soul, a waking angel stirs. Dreams are the seedlings of realities yet to be discovered and explored.

Your circumstances in life may be challenging, but they will not remain so for long if you hold an Ideal and strive to reach it. You cannot journey within and stand still externally.

Consider a young woman raised in poverty and burdened by life. Lacking education and believing herself devoid or worthy talents or skills, she toils long hours in an unhealthy workshop. Yet, she dreams of better things. She dwells on intelligence and focuses her mind on notions of refinement, grace, and beauty. She conceives of, and mentally constructs, an ideal life. A vision of broader liberty and greater scope captivates her, and a restless aspiration propels her into action. She uses all her spare time and resources, limited as they are, to cultivate her latent talents and resources. Soon, her mindset has changed so drastically that the confining workshop can no longer contain her. It has become so out of sync with her mentality that it falls out of her life as easily as one discards an old garment. With the emergence of opportunities that align with her evolving abilities, she leaves it behind forever.

Years later, we see this woman, older and filled with wisdom. She has grasped certain laws of thought, which she wields with confidence, power, and compassion. In her hands, she holds the reins of immense responsibility. She speaks, and lives are transformed in an instant. People hang on to her every word and reshape their characters. Like the sun, she becomes the unwavering and radiant center around which countless destinies revolve. She has actualized the Vision of her youth and become one with her Ideal.

You, too, will realize the vision of your heart, whether it is ordinary or beautiful, or a mix of both, for you will always gravitate towards what you secretly love the most. In your hands will be the tangible results of your thoughts. You will receive what you earn—no more and no less—but the full measure of the effects that you have initiated by setting their underlying causes in motion. Regardless of your current circumstances, you will rise, remain, or fall with your thoughts, your Vision, and your Ideal. You will become as small as your controlling desire or as great as your dominant aspiration.

To borrow the beautiful words of Stanton Kirkham Dave: "You may be keeping accounts, and presently, you will walk out of the door that for so long has seemed to you the barrier of your ideals. You will find yourself before an audience, the pen still behind your ear, ink stains on your fingers, and then and there, the torrent of your inspiration will pour out. You may be driving sheep, and you will wander into the city, wide-eyed and in awe. You will wander under the intrepid guidance of the spirit into the studio of the master, and after a time, that master will say, 'I have nothing more to teach you.' Now you have become the master who once dreamed of great things while driving sheep. You will leave behind your mundane life to take upon yourself the regeneration of the world."

The thoughtless, the uninformed, and the lazy, who see only the superficial effects of things and not the things themselves, speak of luck, fortune, and chance. Seeing a woman grow rich they say, "How lucky she is!" Observing another woman become intellectual or successful in creative pursuits, they exclaim, "How gifted she is!" Seeing the saintly character and far-reaching influence of another, they remark, "How fortune favors her at every turn!" They do not see the trials, the failures, the tireless struggles these women willingly undertook to gain their experience. They know nothing of the sacrifices they made, the unyielding efforts they put forth, the faith they exercised to overcome seemingly insurmountable obstacles and realize the Vision of their hearts. They do not see the darkness and the heartaches; they only see the light and joy, and call it "luck." They do not see the long and arduous journey, but only the pleasant destination, and call it "good fortune." They do not understand the process, but only see the result, and call it "chance."

In all human affairs, there are those who exert effort and those who accomplish their goals. In every instance, the strength of the effort put forth is the measure of the result. Chance is not a factor, and there are no coincidences. What we deem as gifts, talents, possessions, and achievements—whether they be tangible, intellectual, or spiritual—are the outcomes of persistent effort: thoughts completed, goals reached, dreams realized.

The vision that you glorify in your mind, the ideal that you crown in your heart—build your life by this, and you will become the person that embodies them.

Further Insights

This chapter serves as a beacon of light on the horizon, encouraging us not merely to dream but to actively pursue our dreams in the quest for a more rewarding life and a more enlightened world. It underscores the remarkable roles that women, as dreamers and visionaries, have played in shaping our society.

Inspiring women like Frida Kahlo, a renowned Mexican painter whose vibrant artistry imbued the world with beauty and substance; Malala Yousafzai, an activist for female education and the youngest Nobel Prize laureate, who fostered unity and peace; and Jane Goodall, an anthropologist renowned for her work with chimpanzees and her conservation efforts, have all have been architects of a brighter, more hopeful future for humanity. Their stories underscore a compelling truth: when effort is inspired by positive thoughts and actions, it yields rewarding outcomes. Our desires and dreams are not just whimsical thoughts, but signposts on the journey of life and our spiritual destiny.

From childhood, society admonishes us that hard work begets success, and that success is measured by our accumulated wealth. But women like Kahlo, Yousafzai, and Goodall encourage us to question this conventional yardstick of success. Is material wealth truly the ultimate goal?

We must ask ourselves: Are we here in this life to amass material possessions, only to leave them behind when we pass from this world, scattered and forgotten like dust in the wind? When we contemplate the vastness and miracles of the universe, the pursuit of material wealth seems trivial. This realization compels us to look beyond the fleeting illusion of the material world and to focus our gaze on the enduring spiritual realm that lies beyond.

Material wealth loses its allure in the face of failing health. A woman in ill health cannot carry her riches into the next life, nor can she truly enjoy them in this one. Wealth doesn't guarantee happiness; indeed, its obsessive pursuit can lead to suffering, disease, and an unfulfilled life. Wealth cannot awaken us spiritually or lead us to enlightenment; rather, neglecting our spirituality in the pursuit of material goals can stunt our spiritual growth.

Without dreams and goals, we drift aimlessly; however, mere accumulation of material possessions doesn't draw us closer to our true destiny. The physical goals we set for ourselves are stepping stones to something far greater—sometimes, they require us to let go of material possessions to gain something of far greater spiritual value.

A dream or vision offers only a glimpse, not the full picture. This concept is embodied by Mae Jemison, the first African-American woman to travel in space. After accomplishing her initial dream, she continued to contribute to science, technology, and education in various ways, showing that her initial vision was merely the first step of a greater journey. Her story gives us a tantalizing glimpse into possibilities beyond the ordinary, encouraging us to continually expand our horizons.

Never let your dreams be confined by limitations. A woman who perceives her dream as the ultimate destination risks becoming trapped within its limiting boundaries and may never venture beyond.

True visionaries, like the women mentioned above, understand that every dream holds the seed of a grander dream waiting to be realized. Thus, dreams serve as the building blocks of larger aspirations, much like a castle constructed one stone at a time, its final structure a testament to the numerous stones expertly assembled.

To reach a state of happiness, tranquility, and enlightenment, you must continue to dream, to seek knowledge, until the Universe reveals its secrets and you understand the full scope of your vision. This is the pathway to mastery of your destiny, the route to bringing your spiritual garden to full bloom—a timeless pathway many women have walked, and many more are destined to tread.

Chapter 7

Serenity

Calmness of mind is a beautiful jewel of wisdom, a state achieved through persistent and patient effort towards self-control. A calm mind reflects ripened experience and a deep understanding of natural laws and the workings of thought. Attaining this tranquility can be accomplished through various means, including relaxation and meditation. A calm, quiet mind is the first step towards serenity, deep inner peace, and the profound tranquility that accompanies enlightenment.

Your serenity grows as you understand yourself as a thought-evolved being. This awareness also allows you to comprehend and acknowledge others as products of thought. As your understanding deepens and you perceive the interconnectedness of all things more clearly through the actions of cause and effect, you will cease to fuss and fume. You will leave behind anxiety, grief, and fear, recognizing that these agitating forces breed more of the same. When you liberate yourself from this cycle, you'll find it becomes easier to remain poised, steadfast, patient, and serene.

The tranquil woman, having learned to govern herself and adapt to others, radiates dignity, balance, and spiritual strength. Her calmness is noticed and admired by others, who perceive her as a source of reliability and wisdom. She becomes a beacon of calm, her peaceful presence reassuring those around her, thereby reinforcing her own tranquility and peace.

The more tranquil a woman becomes, the greater her success, influence, and power for good. Even one primarily pursuing wealth in business, with no spiritual goals in mind, will find that her prosperity increases as she cultivates self-control and equanimity. People naturally gravitate towards those who project a peaceful and dependable demeanor.

The strong, serene woman is loved and revered by others. She is like a shade-giving tree in a parched land or a sheltering rock in a storm. Who doesn't love a tranquil heart and a balanced life? Regardless of whether it rains or shines, or whatever changes occur, the woman who possesses these blessings remains sublimely positive and serene.

The exquisite state of character known as "serenity" is the ultimate lesson to be mastered in this material world. It is the flowering of life, the fruit of the soul. It is as precious as wisdom, more desirable than fine gold. The pursuit of wealth pales in comparison to a serene life dwelling in the ocean of Truth, beneath the tumultuous waves, beyond the reach of tempests, in the Eternal Calm!

How many people do we know who ruin their

lives and upend all that is sweet and beautiful with explosive tempers? How many create discord and negativity due to a lack of self-control? Sadly, many people wreak havoc in their lives and diminish their happiness through a lack of self-control. It is a rare pleasure to encounter individuals who are well-balanced and possess the exquisite poise that belongs to the calm, serene, and fully evolved character.

Humanity often surges with uncontrolled passion. We are battered by waves of ungoverned grief, blown about by winds of anxiety and doubt. Yet, the calm, strong woman, with her thoughts controlled and uplifted, commands the winds and the storms of the soul to obey her.

To all tempest-tossed souls, regardless of where you are or under what conditions you live, remember this: In the ocean of life, the isles of Blessedness are smiling, and the sunny shore of your Ideal awaits your coming. Keep a firm hand on the helm of your thoughts. In the vessel of your soul reclines the sleeping maker of your circumstances and the architect of your destiny. Wake her! Self-control is strength. Right Thought is mastery. Calmness is power.

Whisper to your heart, "Peace, be still!"

Further Insights

This chapter on *Serenity* reminds us that while wealth can buy comfort, it cannot guarantee peace of mind. As we have discussed previously, you cannot expect to enjoy good health if you persistently sow seeds of unhealthy habits. Knowledge, too, can be elusive if the mind is too distracted or agitated to glean life's nuanced wisdom; the true essence of life often slips away. The path to spiritual tranquility is paved with positive acceptance and release of negativity. Harmonizing with your circumstances allows you to tap into the profound tranquility that prevails in the spiritual realm.

Serenity is a state of mind. The journey to this destination starts with acceptance. Having the wisdom to alter what can be changed and accept what cannot is a guiding light of this path. Cherish the good that graces your life, learn from the challenges, and become the architect of your own destiny. Life is a grand classroom of lessons waiting to be revealed. Acceptance of the transitory nature of the material world and the eternal essence of the soul is the key to unlock the mysteries of eternity and other profound revelations that the universe holds.

When your thoughts are positive and harmonious and your emotions balanced, fears and anxieties dissolve. You stop wrestling with life and rise above failure, knowing that a well-tended garden will inevitably bloom. By setting aside blind ambition, you unleash the true potential of your mind and your higher self—a force that is steady, boundless, and eternal.

A woman with a serene mind and positive thoughts no longer bemoans life's injustices. She understands that challenges and setbacks are fertile soil for life's lessons, without which growth and learning are impossible. Resistance, she knows, is not an adversarial force to be conquered but a catalyst that strengthens her resolve.

A serene mind is in perfect balance and harmony with the universe. This blissful state can only be achieved when you flow with the cosmic tide. In doing so, you'll find yourself at the right place, at the right time, serving your higher purpose, and fulfilling your spiritual destiny. When your life path aligns with your destiny, things fall into place naturally. When you flow with the tide rather than against it, you'll be able to navigate the river of life and realize your true, glorious potential. The light of your soul will radiate brightly, and those around you will be blessed by the warm, healing radiance of your spirit.

Swimming against the tide, on the other hand, will merely exhaust you. Nettles cannot be magically transformed into corn, nor can lead be transmuted into gold. Natural laws are immutable. We can either understand and harness them or disregard and struggle against them.

If you sow fertile seeds with care and diligently tend your garden, you will reap an abundant harvest. But when you grasp the life cycle at work in your garden—that seeds sprout, grow, blossom, and shed their fruits or petals at just the right moment—you become an embodiment of truth, and your life will be blessed with peace and divine love.

In every major philosophy and religion, the importance of serenity is emphasized. The methods to achieve it are numerous and varied: meditation, yoga, visualization, rhythm breathing mantras, affirmations, prayer, and more. Pray or meditate on what is right and pure, and your prayers will be answered. Banish doubt, and you will conquer it. Embrace hope, and your hopes will manifest in reality.

Life is akin to water—it is abundant and free flowing. Your body is the vessel that holds it. Will you let your thoughts churn the water until it spills over? Will you let your emotions stir up the sediment of your doubts and fears? Or will you steady the hand that holds the glass, so that it stays full, and calm your mind so the water remains clear and pure? Every woman must make this choice for herself. Choose wisely. Your health, your happiness, your life, and your spiritual destiny are in your hands.

Chapter 8

Thirty Women Who Changed the World

*A*s I sit down to write the introduction for this final chapter, I can't help but feel a tremendous sense of gratitude. Gratitude for the journey that led me here, to this moment, writing about women who've not just made history, but shaped it—women who tore down walls, shattered glass ceilings, and carved new paths through the wilderness of humanity where none existed before.

This chapter does not appear in the 1903 version of James Allen's classic or any subsequent versions. But I believe it is an essential chapter that must be included in *As a Woman Thinks*, paying tribute to the spirit of women in every time and place throughout history to this moment in time. Were it not for the sacrifices of these women and millions of others who have fought for women's equality and freedom, I would not be able to write this book, or I would be required to put a man's name on it if I wanted it to be published. Thankfully, the world is more enlightened today than at any time in the past, and women are coming into their own. This chapter is a tribute to their undying spirit, an ode to their grit, and a testament to the extraordinary change they've sparked in the world.

The women profiled in this chapter, listed in no particular order, came from all corners of the globe, from different times, cultures, and backgrounds. Some were born into privilege, while others clawed their way up from the depths of poverty. Their stories are as different as they are compelling, but one thread binds them all—a relentless pursuit of their purpose, a fiery determination to fulfill their destiny, and a courage that saw them stand tall when faced with seemingly insurmountable odds.

Each of the thirty women profiled in this chapter carved their initials on the world, a mark that time and tide cannot wash away. Their names echo in the pages of history, inspiring generation after generation of girls and women who dream of blazing their own trails and leaving their own marks. These women challenged norms, defied conventions, and time and time again proved that "impossible" is just a word that can limit our hopes and imaginations.

In this chapter, we travel back through time to meet queens and scientists, writers and activists, artists and astronauts—each with a unique tale to tell. We delve briefly into their lives, their struggles, and their legacies. Filled with trials and triumphs, their life journeys are as inspiring as they are enlightening. These stories are a testament to the indomitable spirit of women—their power, their resilience, their grace.

Of course, the women mentioned here represent only a handful of the untold millions who have shaped history and continue to do so today in their own extraordinary ways. Every woman, including you, has the power to create or effect change, in their lives, in their surroundings, and in the lives of others. Their contributions, their choices, and their sacrifices, no matter how consequential or mundane, are potentially life-changing and certainly worthy of recognition.

These women are not merely names and faces in the pages of history—they are eternal beacons that remind us of the power that resides within every woman—the power to question, to challenge, to change, to create. The power to dream, and not just dream, but to bring those dreams to life. All of these women were once just girls, no different than you or I, with their own hopes and dreams, fears, and doubts. Yet, they rose. They fought, they learned, they failed, and they stood up again, refusing to be sidelined, silenced, minimized, or defeated.

So, this chapter isn't just about thirty women who changed the world—it's an invitation, a call for every woman reading this book to harness her potential, tap into her strength, and carve out her own place in the world. Let the lives and stories of these women be an inspiration for all of us, regardless of our chosen paths. It is through our collective efforts, diverse aspirations, and mutual support that we can continue to shape a world where every woman's voice is heard, valued, and respected. Let us celebrate the achievements of women and strive to create a future where we all can thrive and make their mark on the world!

Marie Curie: Amidst a repressive regime in Poland that thwarted women's education, Marie Curie had to resort to clandestine means to pursue her studies, attending an underground university. Her grit catapulted her to become the first woman to win a Nobel Prize, and she remains the only person to have received this prestigious award in two distinct fields—physics and chemistry. Her groundbreaking discoveries of radium and polonium, and her pioneering research on radioactivity, laid the foundation for momentous advancements in science and medicine, including the development of X-rays. Despite facing gender bias in academia, Curie's dedication set a powerful precedent for future generations of aspiring women scientists. Today, her enduring legacy illuminates the realms of medicine and nuclear physics, affirming the potential for women to excel in science.

Rosa Parks: During an era overshadowed by racial discrimination, Rosa Parks became a beacon of hope for the American Civil Rights Movement. Her defiant refusal to yield her seat on a segregated bus to a white passenger ignited the Montgomery Bus Boycott, a pivotal moment in the fight against racial segregation. Parks stayed resolute in her commitment to racial equality despite death threats and the loss of her job. Her courage kindled a flame of resistance that motivated many to challenge racial inequality head-on. Today, her actions resonate in significant civil rights legislation in the United States, providing stronger legal protection against discrimination and benefiting women of color in particular.

Florence Nightingale: Known as "the Lady with the Lamp," Florence Nightingale defied societal norms that restricted women to domestic roles, carving out a path as a nursing pioneer. She instigated groundbreaking improvements to hospital sanitation during the Crimean War, resulting in a dramatic reduction in patient mortality rates. Despite encountering skepticism and resistance, Nightingale founded the first scientifically based nursing school, igniting a transformative shift in the nursing profession. While her dedication to nursing and hospital reform often conflicted with military and medical officials, it laid the groundwork for modern nursing practices. Nightingale's commitment to professionalizing nursing has since opened doors for countless women in healthcare, a field where women now constitute the majority of the workforce.

Amelia Earhart: In an era where women were largely consigned to domestic roles, Amelia Earhart defied societal expectations and gravity itself by becoming the first woman to fly solo across the Atlantic Ocean. Her audacious plunge into the male-dominated world of aviation served as a guiding light for other women, proving they could attain unprecedented heights. Earhart's trailblazing achievements in aviation, in spite of societal skepticism and doubts about women's capabilities in technical fields, paved the way for an influx of women in the industry. Her legacy continues to inspire many women to pursue careers in aeronautics and other technical disciplines.

Frida Kahlo: Faced with severe health challenges, including polio during her childhood and a nearly fatal bus accident in her adolescence, Frida Kahlo transformed her personal pain into emotionally resonant and symbolically rich artwork. Her incisive explorations of identity, gender, class, and race provided a vivid and poignant portrayal of the female experience, establishing her as one of the most celebrated painters of her time. Personal hardships, including a tumultuous relationship with her husband Diego Rivera and a heartbreaking miscarriage, deeply influenced her art, often manifesting in themes of pain and suffering. Kahlo's enduring legacy continues to inspire countless women to express their personal experiences through art, contributing to a more diverse and inclusive representation in the world of art.

Mother Teresa: Emerging from humble beginnings, Mother Teresa was drawn to serve the destitute from an early age. Leaving her home in Macedonia, she joined the Sisters of Loreto in Ireland before relocating to India, where she confronted the harsh realities of poverty. Her unwavering commitment to aiding the poor, the sick, and the dying earned her the Nobel Peace Prize, leaving an indelible imprint on global humanitarian endeavors. Despite daily encounters with poverty, disease, and death, Mother Teresa remained determined to make a difference. Her selfless devotion continues to inspire those committed to humanitarian efforts and has significantly improved the lives of some of the world's most vulnerable, particularly impoverished women.

Eleanor Roosevelt: Navigating the societal constraints and expectations of the early 20th century, Eleanor Roosevelt transformed the First Lady's role from a primarily ceremonial one into a powerful platform for advocacy, championing human rights and social justice. Even after her tenure in the White House, she remained a tireless advocate for global human rights, playing a pivotal role in the drafting of the Universal Declaration of Human Rights. Despite personal trials, including her husband's polio diagnosis and intense public scrutiny that accompanied her role, Roosevelt persistently championed civil rights and women's issues, effecting lasting social and political changes. Her work, particularly her contributions to the Universal Declaration of Human Rights, continues to shape international human rights law, positively impacting women worldwide.

Emmeline Pankhurst: Born into an era when women were treated as second-class citizens and denied fundamental voting rights, Emmeline Pankhurst courageously defied societal norms and public contempt. She founded and led the Women's Social and Political Union, a suffragette organization known for its militant tactics. Pankhurst's commitment to women's suffrage often put her at odds with the law, leading to multiple arrests and prison time. Despite facing violent opposition and brutal force-feeding during prison hunger strikes, she remained resolute in her mission. Her determined efforts significantly contributed to women securing the right to vote in the UK, marking a critical milestone towards gender equality. Today, her enduring legacy continues to inspire women's rights movements worldwide.

Ada Lovelace: Recognized as the world's first computer programmer, Ada Lovelace's groundbreaking work on Charles Babbage's early mechanical computer—the Analytical Engine—was unquestionably visionary. Her notes included what is considered the first algorithm intended to be processed by a machine. In defiance of societal norms that discouraged women's involvement in scientific and mathematical fields, Lovelace shattered barriers. She envisioned the creative potential of machines beyond mere calculations and foresaw their application in areas like art and music. Though her pioneering contributions in the male-dominated fields of mathematics and computer science went largely unrecognized during her lifetime, today, her achievements are celebrated worldwide. In particular, Ada Lovelace Day—an international event observed on October 13—aims to highlight the accomplishments of women in STEM fields and inspire girls interested in science, technology, engineering, and mathematics. Lovelace's enduring legacy stands as a testament to women's significant contributions to computing history and as an inspiration for future generations to follow their passions.

Harriet Tubman: Born into slavery, Harriet Tubman escaped her captors and courageously served as a "conductor" on the Underground Railroad, risking her life repeatedly to guide dozens of enslaved people to freedom. Amid a period of rampant racial prejudice and legalized slavery, Tubman emerged as a beacon of hope, fighting tirelessly for human rights and dignity. Despite the severe hardships and dangers she encountered while working with the Underground Railroad and later as Union Army cook and scout during the Civil War, Tubman exhibited remarkable courage and strength. Her legacy continues to inspire civil rights and social justice movements today and serves as a powerful testament to the ongoing struggle against racial oppression.

Joan of Arc: Born a peasant in medieval France, Joan of Arc defied societal norms, gender expectations, and even accusations of heresy to lead the French army to several pivotal victories during the Hundred Years' War, a bitter conflict between England and France—all before her eighteenth birthday. Inspired by her faith, she attributed her heroism and remarkable military successes to divine guidance. Yet despite her battlefield triumphs, Joan faced skepticism, betrayal, and ultimately execution by the English at just 19 years old. Her unwavering faith and bravery led to her canonization centuries later as a patron saint of France. Today, her enduring legacy continues to inspire millions, particularly women confronting gender-based discrimination in traditionally male-dominated fields, serving as a testament to the power of conviction and courage.

Hatshepsut: One of the few female pharaohs of Ancient Egypt, Hatshepsut challenged societal norms and courtly objections to rule for over two decades during Egypt's 18th Dynasty. Her reign saw the expansion of trade routes, the initiation of monumental building projects, and sustained peace, contributing to a prosperous legacy. Despite her accomplishments, Hatshepsut faced internal opposition due to her gender and often adopted masculine portrayals in statues and artwork to reinforce her authority. Tragically, many of her monuments and statues were defaced or destroyed after her death in an attempt to erase her from history. Nonetheless, Hatshepsut's reign, one of the most successful in Ancient Egyptian history, stands as a powerful example of female leadership, inspiring modern women who occupy or aspire to leadership roles.

Helen Keller: Despite losing her sight and hearing to illness as a young child, Helen Keller emerged as a celebrated writer, speaker, and advocate for individuals with disabilities. With the guidance of her teacher, Anne Sullivan, she overcame the isolation imposed by her disabilities and societal indifference using a system of tactile sign language. Beyond transforming widely held perceptions of disability through her relentless perseverance and determination, Keller also co-founded the American Civil Liberties Union (ACLU), extending her impact beyond disability advocacy. Despite skepticism and prejudice, she devoted her life to advocating for the rights of the disabled. Today, Keller's legacy continues to shape recognition and rights for people with disabilities, offering invaluable inspiration to contemporary women facing similar challenges.

Valentina Tereshkova: At a time when many women were just entering the workforce, Valentina Tereshkova, a factory worker and amateur skydiver, shattered the ultimate glass ceiling by becoming the first woman in space in 1963. This extraordinary personal achievement marked a symbolic victory for all women during the early Space Age. Despite enduring a grueling training regimen and the inherent risks of space travel, Tereshkova's journey stands as a powerful testament to women's capabilities in fields traditionally dominated by men. Her groundbreaking achievement continues to inspire future generations of female astronauts and women in STEM fields.

Indira Gandhi: As India's first and only female prime minister to date, Indira Gandhi navigated the male-dominated landscape of Indian politics, leading the country for fifteen years. Despite staunch opposition from her own party and the broader political arena, she implemented progressive policies and demonstrated remarkable courage and resilience until her assassination in 1984. During her tenure, Gandhi faced numerous political and personal adversities, including a declared state of emergency, corruption allegations, the tragic loss of her son, and the Indo-Pakistani War of 1971. Despite these challenges, she led with resolute courage and strength. Today, Gandhi's leadership continues to inspire contemporary women in politics, serving as a vivid example of women's potential to lead in traditionally male-dominated arenas.

Coco Chanel: Gabrielle Bonheur Chanel, famously known as Coco Chanel, emerged from a traumatic childhood as an orphan in a poor family to revolutionize the fashion world. She defied societal norms by introducing comfortable and practical designs for women, including trousers, her iconic "little black dresses," and the signature Chanel suit. Despite controversy surrounding her during World War II due to her associations with the Nazi-German occupiers, Chanel's influence extended beyond fashion, reaching to jewelry, handbags, and fragrance. Her lasting impact on the fashion industry continues to resonate today.

Simone de Beauvoir: Born into a bourgeois Parisian family, Simone de Beauvoir emerged as a prominent existentialist philosopher, feminist, and social theorist. Her seminal work, *The Second Sex,* is a critical analysis of women's oppression and has become a cornerstone of modern feminism. Despite societal pushback and the loss of her teaching job due to allegations of sexual misconduct, de Beauvoir's insightful analysis of women's oppression and her advocacy for gender equality profoundly influenced feminist theory and the women's rights movement.

Margaret Sanger: In an era when birth control was a taboo subject, Margaret Sanger bravely confronted societal and legal conventions to educate women about contraception. Unfazed by arrests and exile, she opened the first birth control clinic in the United States, and founded organizations that evolved into Planned Parenthood. Sanger encountered fierce opposition from religious and political groups, facing censorship and denouncement. Despite these challenges, her pioneering work revolutionized women's access to reproductive healthcare and empowered them to make informed choices about their bodies and family planning, leaving a lasting legacy on women's reproductive rights.

Sacagawea:. A Lemhi Shoshone woman, Sacagawea navigated through a life fraught with hardship, including abduction and enslavement by an opposing tribe. She played a vital role in the historic Lewis and Clark expedition, offering invaluable navigation and negotiation assistance with other tribes, all while caring for her newborn son. Despite language barriers, dangerous terrains, and cultural prejudices, Sacagawea's significant contributions to the expedition underscored the strength and resilience of indigenous women and highlighted their crucial role in American history.

Rachel Carson: As a marine biologist and conservationist, Rachel Carson weathered industry backlash and personal health challenges to expose the dangers of pesticide use in her groundbreaking book, *Silent Spring*. Despite fierce criticism from chemical companies and powerful interest groups, her work led to a nationwide ban on DDT and the establishment of the U.S. Environmental Protection Agency. Carson's legacy as a pioneer of the environmental movement continues to inspire conservation efforts and environmental activism. Her work also underscored the vital role of women's voices in science and conservation, breaking barriers and inspiring more female scientists to engage in environmental research and activism.

Sojourner Truth: Born into slavery, Truth made her escape to freedom with her infant daughter and later emerged as a resolute advocate for abolition, women's rights, and prison reform. Using her experiences as a springboard, she confronted racial and gender discrimination head-on. Despite suffering severe hardships, including the loss of her son to slavery, Truth's legacy has been instrumental in spurring critical discussions on the interconnectedness of racial and gender discrimination, providing a substantial contribution to modern discourse on women's rights.

Marie Stopes: A pioneer in family planning, Stopes faced and successfully navigated significant legal resistance and opposition from the medical community when she established Britain's first birth control clinic. Despite facing widespread criticism and personal challenges, including a controversial divorce, Stopes' advocacy played a crucial role in normalizing contraception and reshaping prevailing attitudes towards women's reproductive rights. Her work has continued to empower modern women by granting them more control over their reproductive choices.

Wangari Maathai: Overcoming gender bias and political persecution, Maathai became the first

African woman to win the Nobel Peace Prize for her contributions to sustainable development, democracy, and peace. She founded the Green Belt Movement, which has planted over 51 million trees and has empowered thousands of women with new skills and income sources. Maathai's resistance to political and economic forces exploiting natural resources without considering the destructive effects on local communities underscores the crucial role of women's empowerment in sustainable development and environmental stewardship.

Boudica: As queen of the British Celtic Iceni tribe, Boudica led a rebellion against the occupying forces of the Roman Empire when they denied her claim to her husband's throne and violated her daughters. Despite her eventual defeat, her revolt made a significant impact and has endured in English folklore. Facing numerous challenges in a male-dominated society, Boudica's resistance against Roman rule continues to inspire subsequent generations, symbolizing steadfast resistance against oppression. Her legacy serves as a testament to the strength and resilience of women throughout history.

Malala Yousafzai: At the young age of fifteen, Malala survived an assassination attempt by the Taliban for advocating for girls' education in Pakistan. Since then, she has amplified her activism on a global scale, becoming the youngest Nobel laureate and inspiring countless young people to champion their rights. Despite risking her life, Yousafzai spoke out against the suppression of girls' education in her region. Her unwavering courage and determination highlight the transformative power of education as a catalyst for change and continue to empower young girls worldwide to fight for their right to education and equality.

Ruth Bader Ginsburg: As one of a mere handful of women studying law in the 1950s, Ruth Bader Ginsburg overcame significant discrimination to graduate law school and rise to prominence as a Supreme Court Justice and a feminist icon. She tirelessly worked to combat gender-based stereotypes and legal barriers that perpetuated gender inequality. Her legacy extends to shaping landmark court decisions that advanced reproductive rights, equal pay, and LGBTQ+ rights, thus strengthening the foundation of gender equality in the United States.

Cleopatra: As the last dynastic pharaoh of Egypt's Ptolemaic Kingdom, Cleopatra showcased her aptitude as a skilled diplomat, naval commander, and medical author. Against a backdrop of political turmoil in a patriarchal society, she managed to maintain her rule and preserve Egypt's independence. Her enduring legacy has profoundly influenced perceptions of powerful women, challenging traditional gender norms and illuminating the potential of female leadership.

Elizabeth I: Ascending to the throne in a time of political and religious unrest, Elizabeth I faced many challenges, including gender-based opposition. Her forty-four-year reign, known as the Elizabethan era, saw the flourishing of English drama, exploration, and naval power, cementing her place among England's most notable monarchs. Demonstrating the capabilities of a female ruler to lead effectively and inspire cultural and economic growth, Elizabeth's legacy continues to empower women and pave the way for future generations of female leaders.

Maya Angelou: Growing up in the segregated American South, Maya Angelou experienced pervasive racism and systemic inequalities, as well as the trauma of childhood sexual abuse. Despite these adversities, she emerged as a trailblazing figure in literature and an influential voice for women's rights and racial equality. Her writings, including her acclaimed memoir, *I Know Why the Caged Bird Sings,* have inspired women worldwide, providing a platform for marginalized voices and illuminating the intersectionality of race and gender to foster a broader understanding.

Susan B. Anthony: As a 19th-century women's rights activist, Susan B. Anthony withstood public ridicule and legal persecution for her advocacy. Her act of civil disobedience—voting illegally in the 1872 presidential election—brought attention to the denial of women's suffrage rights. She was arrested and found guilty at trial by a hostile judge who denied her the right to testify on her own behalf. Despite the guilty verdict and fine, which she refused to pay, Anthony's relentless pursuit of women's rights was instrumental in the passage of the 19th amendment to the U.S. Constitution, granting women the right to vote. Anthony's courage and determination laid the groundwork for the modern feminist movement, expanding political opportunities for women and advancing gender equality in the United States and beyond.

—The End...And Your New Beginning!—

About the Author

Abby Leigh Hunter grew up near the cornfields of the Midwest, reading everything she could get her hands on. From her mother's latest copies of *Cosmopolitan* and *Reader's Digest* to her grandmother's stacks of *The Star* and other supermarket tabloids, Abby developed a deep love of reading and a desire to share and talk about the amazing things she learned, which not surprisingly led to an interest in writing.

Abby spent her days in school reading the latest novels that caught her interest or writing poems and letters to friends instead of taking in her lessons. Her "too cool for school" attitude did not reflect well on her grades, but it did provide a creative outlet that would shape her adult life. Fascinated by the enduring tales the world's great authors of past and present could weave, she aspired to study them and one day write stories just as extraordinary. She became fascinated with classics, which led to an editor's role with a small educational publisher, where her credits include academic editions of classics by Oscar Wilde and H.P. Lovecraft.

Abby resides in a sleepy village on California's scenic central coast with her husband (a lifelong writer and editor), their cat, and a yard full of blooming flowers and happy birds. She enjoys cliches, sunsets, long walks on the beach, and she will always love a good book.

Other Books by this Author:

Seasons Change, Life Gets Better
Abby Leigh Hunter (author)
Formats: e-book, paperback, hardcover

The Picture of Dorian Gray (Academic Edition)
Oscar Wilde (Author); Abby Leigh Hunter (Editor)
Formats: e-book, paperback, hardcover

The Picture of Dorian Gray: Study Guide & Workbook
Abby Leigh Hunter (Author)
Formats: e-book, paperback, hardcover

At the Mountains of Madness (Academic Edition)
H.P. Lovecraft (Author); Abby Leigh Hunter (Editor)
Formats: e-book, paperback, hardcover

The Whisperer in Darkness (Academic Edition)
H.P. Lovecraft (Author); Abby Leigh Hunter (Editor)
Formats: e-book, paperback, hardcover

The Dunwich Horror (Academic Edition)
H.P. Lovecraft (Author); Abby Leigh Hunter (Editor)
Formats: e-book, paperback, hardcover

Notes

Notes

Notes

www.ingramcontent.com/pod-product-compliance
Lightning Source LLC
Chambersburg PA
CBHW060405080526
44583CB00012B/473